Union Club of Boston

The Constitution, By-laws and House Rules of the Union Club of Boston

Union Club of Boston

The Constitution, By-laws and House Rules of the Union Club of Boston

ISBN/EAN: 9783337157715

Printed in Europe, USA, Canada, Australia, Japan

Cover: Foto ©ninafisch / pixelio.de

More available books at **www.hansebooks.com**

THE

CONSTITUTION

BY-LAWS AND HOUSE RULES

OF THE

UNION CLUB

OF BOSTON

WITH A LIST OF THE OFFICERS AND MEMBERS

JULY 1885.

THE Constitution and By-Laws of the Union Club as printed in this edition are the same as in the edition of 1883, which was verified and corrected by comparison with the original records.

HENRY W. SWIFT,

Secretary.

JULY, 1885.

INDEX.

HOUSE RULES.

LIST OF OFFICERS AND MEMBERS.

PREAMBLE.

THE UNION CLUB OF BOSTON was founded in the year 1863 for "the encouragement and dissemination of patriotic sentiment and opinion," and the condition of membership was "unqualified loyalty to the Constitution and the Union of the United States, and unwavering support of the Federal Government in efforts for the suppression of the Rebellion."

Its organization is continued to promote social intercourse and to afford the conveniences of a Club House.

CONSTITUTION.

I.

NAME.

THIS Club shall be called the UNION CLUB OF BOSTON.

II.

MEMBERS.

Any person duly elected a member shall, upon signing an agreement to observe the Constitution and By-Laws, and paying his entrance-fee and the annual assessment, or, if elected after the first day of July in any year, the entrance-fee and half of the annual assessment, become thenceforth entitled to all the rights and privileges of membership, provided such acts shall be performed within three months from the date of such election. Persons elected members of the Club during the month of December in any year shall not be required to pay any assessment for that year. The number of members of the Club, resident and non-resident, shall not be increased by election so as to exceed five hundred at any one time.

III.

PROPERTY.

The title to the real estate held for the use and benefit of the Club shall remain in the Trustees to whom the same was conveyed by deed dated Feb. 1, 1868, and recorded in Suffolk Registry of Deeds, Lib. 919, Fol. 148, for the uses and purposes set forth in their Declaration of Trust recorded in the said Registry with the deed aforesaid. The legal title and ownership of all the other property, effects, and assets of the Club shall be in the Executive Committee for the time being, in trust for the benefit and enjoyment of the members.

IV.

GOVERNMENT.

The officers of the Club shall be a President, four Vice-Presidents, eight Directors, a Treasurer, and a Secretary, who shall constitute the Executive Committee of the Club. They shall be elected at the Annual Meeting in December, and shall hold office for one year from the first day of January following, and until their successors shall have been chosen and shall have accepted office. The President, or in his absence the Senior Vice-President in the order of election, shall preside at all meetings of the Club and of the Executive Committee ; and, if the President and all the Vice-

Presidents shall be absent, a chairman shall be chosen by vote.

If the office of the President or of the Treasurer shall become vacant, the Executive Committee shall call a special meeting of the Club to fill such vacancy. If any other vacancy shall occur, the Executive Committee may fill the same.

BY-LAWS.

I.

EXECUTIVE COMMITTEE.

The Executive Committee shall have the management and control of the Club and of its property, and shall exercise a general superintendence of its interests and affairs. They may make or authorize all necessary contracts, but shall have no power to make the Club liable for any debt beyond the amount of money which shall, at the time of contracting such debt, be in the Treasurer's hands, and not needed for the discharge of prior debts or liabilities. They shall have power to make such regulations and rules for the domestic and internal economy, comfort, and success of the establishment as they shall think proper; and, generally, to do all things which may be necessary for the proper management of its concerns.

They shall appoint from their number a House Committee of five, who shall control the expenses and charges of the Club, regulate prices, receive and redress complaints, and have the immediate charge and superintendence of the Club, subject, however, at all times, to the direction of the Executive Committee. The House Committee shall have power, subject always to the control of the Executive Committee, to engage and discharge the servants of the Club, to make necessary purchases and sales, and to enforce the preservation of order, and obedience to the Constitution and By-Laws.

II.

MEETINGS OF EXECUTIVE COMMITTEE.

The Executive Committee, of which five shall be a quorum, shall hold stated meetings during the first week of every month,— July, August, and September excepted,— for the transaction of business ; and special meetings may be called by the Secretary, on request of the President or any Vice-President, or of any two Directors, upon notice, printed or written, to be given to each member at least twenty-four hours before the time appointed for such meeting.

The House Committee shall hold meetings on Monday evening of each week, at eight o'clock.

III.

TREASURER.

The Treasurer shall be charged with the collection and custody of the funds of the Club, and their disbursement under the direction of the House Committee. He shall keep the accounts of the Club in books belonging to it, and shall exhibit his account at the Annual Meeting, and shall present a copy thereof to such auditors as shall be appointed by the Club to examine it, who shall make their report thereon to the Executive Committee at their next stated monthly meeting, or as soon thereafter as conveniently may be; and, if the same shall be approved by the Committee, such account shall be deemed thenceforth conclusively settled. If it be not approved, the same shall be submitted to the Club at any subsequent stated meeting, or special meeting called to act thereupon. His books shall be at all times open to the inspection of any member of the Executive Committee; and he may be removed by the Club or the Committee, at any time, for refusal to exhibit them, or for any misconduct in the affairs of his office. The Committee may authorize him to employ such assistance as it shall think proper, at the expense of the Club, in the keeping of his books and preparing of his accounts and reports. He shall be exempted from payment of the annual assessment.

IV.

SECRETARY.

The Secretary shall keep a record of all the meetings of the Club, and of the proceedings of the Executive Committee, and of the Committee on Elections; and shall have the custody of all the documents of the Club, shall conduct its correspondence, and have the superintendence of its library, magazines, and newspapers. He shall be exempted from payment of the annual assessment.

V.

ELECTION OF MEMBERS.

There shall be a Committee on Elections, consisting of the Secretary and fourteen other members of the Club, who shall be elected by ballot at the Annual Meeting, and any vacancy in whose number may be filled by the Committee. Meetings of the Committee shall be held on the first Tuesday after the first Saturday of every month, except July, August, and September.

Whenever any person shall be proposed for membership, written application must be made by a member of the Club to the Committee on Elections, subscribed by him, setting forth the name and place of residence of the person proposed, and the date of such proposal. If a majority of the Committee shall deem him a suitable person for membership, they shall cause his name to be placed on the notice-board, as a candidate for admission, for the space of ten days.

All elections shall be by secret ballot: thirty votes shall be necessary to constitute a ballot on each nomination ; and one-fifth part of the votes being in the negative shall constitute a rejection. The ballot-box shall be kept in the custody of the clerk at the office. Printed or written lists of the candidates to be balloted for shall be placed in the hands of the clerk, for the use of the members; which ballots may be deposited in the box at any time after the nomination, until the ballot shall be closed. Each member may write Yes or No against any names on his ballot; and his vote shall not be counted for or against any candidate not thus marked. The balloting shall be closed at seven o'clock of the evening of the tenth day thereof, and the votes shall be counted by two members of the Executive Committee, who shall report the result of the election to the Committee on Elections, and the Secretary shall enter the same on the records of the Club, and shall post on the notice-board a list of the candidates elected. No one but the Committee who count the votes, the Secretary, and the clerk shall, on any account, see the list of members who have so voted. No candidate who shall have been rejected shall be again proposed within six months.

VI.

NON-RESIDENT MEMBERS.

Persons who do not reside within forty miles of Boston, and have no place of business there, may be admitted to membership in the Club upon payment of half the rates of entrance-fees and annual assessments; provided that it shall be set forth, in the application to the Committee on Elections for the nomination of a non-resident candidate, that he belongs to such class; and provided also that, when any non-resident member shall cease to belong to that class, by residing within forty miles of Boston or having a place of business there, he shall thereupon be liable to pay the residue of the entrance-fee, and, thereafter, to pay full annual assessments. Non-resident members shall have all the rights and privileges of resident members, except that, in the event of a dissolution of the Club, the interest of a non-resident member in its property and assets shall be a .half share only.

After Oct. 1, 1883, there shall be no further election of non-resident members under this By-Law.

VII.

ARMY AND NAVY MEMBERS.

Any officer of the Army or Navy of the United States on duty within the New England States may be admitted to the use of the Club, in the manner provided for the election of members, upon his paying half the annual assessment, which shall entitle him to the privileges of membership for six months, and a like sum in advance for each additional term of six months, or part thereof, during which he shall so remain on duty and continue to use the Club ; and he will be assessed at the beginning of each term of six months, unless he shall have previously given notice to the Treasurer of his intention to discontinue using the Club ; but he shall not have the right of voting, and, in the event of the dissolution of the Club, he shall have no interest in its property.

VIII.

RESIGNATIONS.

All resignations shall be made in writing, addressed to the Executive Committee, on or before the thirty-first day of December ; and any resignation made subsequently thereto shall not discharge the member presenting it from his assessment for the ensuing year. Such resignation shall operate as an assignment and release to the Executive Committee, as Trustees of the Club, of all the right, title, and interest of such member in and to the property and assets of the Club.

IX.

FORFEITURE OF MEMBERSHIP.

Any three members may present to the Executive Committee written charges subscribed by themselves against any other member ; and, if it shall appear to the Executive Committee on inquiry, after notice to the member so charged and an opportunity given him to be heard in his defence, that his conduct has endangered or is likely to endanger the good order, welfare, or character of the Club, or is at variance with the requirements of the Constitution and By-Laws, the Executive Committee may, by vote of two-thirds of its members, suspend such member, or declare his membership forfeited. The member thus suspended or expelled shall have the right, within one month after receiving notification of such action, to appeal to the members of the Club. The President, or, in case of his absence, one of the Vice-Presidents, shall thereupon call a special meeting of the Club, to be held within one month after he is notified of such appeal. If two-thirds of the members present at such meeting shall by secret ballot reverse the action of the Executive Committee, the appellant shall be restored to member-ship; but, until such reversal, he shall not be entitled to any of the privileges of a member. A forfeiture shall operate to vest in the Executive Committee, as Trustees of the Club, all the right, title, and interest of such expelled member in and to the property and assets thereof.

X.

STRANGERS.

All persons not members of the Club, who reside forty miles or more beyond the limits of the city of Boston and have no place of business therein, shall be deemed strangers.

The Executive Committee may, by vote, extend the privileges of the House to any stranger during his visit to the city, and any member of the Committee may, at the written request of any member of the Club, issue a written invitation to any stranger, conferring such privileges for not more than one month; but no such invitation shall be issued to a stranger who has re-ceived a similar invitation within three months, unless by a vote of either the Executive Committee or House Committee.

Any member may introduce a stranger into the Club House for one day only, but such introduction shall not confer a right of entrance except on that day.

Other persons not members may be introduced into the House not oftener than once in three months, unless to an entertainment given by a member in a private room.

The member introducing or requesting an invitation for any person not a member shall register, in a book to be kept in the office of the Club for that purpose, his name and residence and the date of the introduction or request, and shall add thereto his own name ; but this provision for registration shall not apply to a person introduced into a private room.

No guest shall have the right to bring any person into the House ; and it shall be in the power of either the Executive Committee or House Committee to exclude any person not a member, whenever they may consider it advisable to do so.

XI.

ASSESSMENTS.

To defray the current ordinary expenses of the Club, and to provide for the payment of the certificates of indebtedness issued for the purchase of the Club House, there shall be an entrance-fee of one hundred dollars paid by each new member, and an annual assessment of fifty dollars paid by each member.

The annual assessment shall be payable on the first day of January, of which written or printed notice shall be given by the Treasurer to each member, through the post-office, on or before that day; and it shall be the duty of the Treasurer to report the names of all members delinquent on the first day of March to the Executive Committee at their next monthly meeting for such action thereon as they may deem expedient; and the Committee may declare the membership of any such delinquent member forfeited.

XII.

MEETINGS OF THE CLUB.

The Annual Meeting of the Club shall be holden on the third Saturday of December, at eight o'clock P.M., for the choice of officers, and all other business that may be brought before it. Notices of meetings shall be posted on the notice-board by the Secretary for at least ten days before the times assigned for them respectively; and written or printed notice of the Annual Meeting, addressed to each member, shall be deposited in the post-office at least ten days before the time thereof.

At any meeting of the Club for an alteration of the Constitution or By-Laws, or for action on an appeal from a decision of the Executive Committee suspending or expelling a member, sixty members shall constitute a quorum; for the transaction of any other business, thirty members shall be a quorum.

At all meetings, discussions shall be limited to matters affecting the interests of the Club; and it shall never be called upon or permitted to act, in its official or associate capacity as a club, upon any political question or subject.

No stranger or visitor shall be present at any meeting.

XIII.

PROXIES.

Voting by proxy shall be allowed in the transaction of any business of the Club, except in elections and on appeals from the action of the Executive Committee.

XIV.

ANNUAL MEETING.

At the Annual Meeting, the Executive Committee, Treasurer, and Secretary shall make full reports of their proceedings for the past year, and recommend such measures as they deem advisable. The order of business shall be as follows : —

1. Reading the minutes of the preceding meeting.

2. Report of the Executive Committee. '

3. Report of the Treasurer, and appointment of Auditors.

4. Report of the Secretary.

5. Election of officers for the ensuing year.

6. Any further business regularly before the meeting.

Provided, however, that the order may be changed by a vote of the majority of those present.

XV.

SPECIAL MEETINGS.

A special meeting shall be called whenever the Executive Committee shall consider one expedient, or whenever twenty-five members not of the Committee shall, in writing, setting forth the purpose thereof, request the President or any Vice-President to call one ; and notice of any such meeting shall be posted on the notice-board for at least ten days before the time assigned therefor, setting forth the matter intended to be acted upon; and no business other than that specified in the notice shall be acted upon at such special meeting.

XVI.

NOMINATIONS AND ELECTIONS.

A meeting of the Club shall be held on the third Saturday of October in each year, at eight o'clock P.M., when a committee of seven members shall be chosen to nominate candidates for office for the ensuing year. The Committee shall make their report to the Secre-

tary on or before the third Saturday of the following
month, and he shall cause a printed list of the candidates nominated to be placed upon the notice-board at
least ten days before the Annual Meeting.

All elections of officers shall be by ballot, unless
otherwise ordered by two-thirds of the members present ; and a plurality of votes shall constitute an election.

XVII.

HOUSE OPEN.

The House shall be open for the reception of members every day, under such rules and regulations as the
Executive Committee may prescribe.

XVIII.

SERVANTS.

No member or visitor shall give any money or gra-
tuity to any servant of the Club ; and no servant shall
be employed by any member on any business of his
own, out of the Club House, without permission of the
superintendent or clerk.

XIX.

PAYMENT OF DUES.

All indebtedness of members to the Club, other than
for assessments, shall be paid on or before the first day
of every month.   And if, at the expiration of the four-

teenth day of any month, any member shall not have
paid his dues to the Club for the preceding month, he
shall receive no further credit until such dues are paid.
It shall be the duty of the clerk, upon the fifteenth day
of each month, to post in some conspicuous place in
the Club House the names of all members whose dues
are then unpaid, together with the amount due from
each member, there to remain until the same are paid.
The Executive Committee may at any meeting declare
forfeited the membership of any member whose name
and the amount due from him having been posted as
aforesaid shall have remained posted forty-five days,
provided such amount or some part thereof shall remain unpaid at the time of such meeting.

XX.

INJURY TO CLUB PROPERTY.

Any destruction of the property of the Club, or in-
jury to it, shall be paid for by the member who shall
have caused the same ; and the amount to be paid shall
be determined by the House Committee.

XXI.

AMENDMENTS OF CONSTITUTION AND BY-LAWS.

Alterations of the Constitution and By-Laws may be
made at the Annual Meeting, or at the regular October
meeting, provided written notice of the proposed alteration shall have been given to the Secretary, and a

copy thereof filed with him, and posted by him on the notice-board for at least ten days before the meeting. They may also be made at any special meeting called for the purpose, and notified in the manner directed in Article XV. In either case, the assent of two-thirds of the members present shall be necessary.

HOUSE RULES

I.

HOURS OF OPENING AND CLOSING.

The House shall be open for the reception of members every day from eight A.M. until half-past one A.M., except on Sunday, when the House shall be closed at midnight.

The dining-room shall be open for meals to be served, daily, from eight A.M. until midnight.

II.

BOOKS AND PAMPHLETS.

No person shall take from the Club House any book, pamphlet, newspaper, or other article belonging to the Club, or mutilate or destroy the same.

III.

SMOKING.

Smoking is prohibited in the dining-room, and in the smaller front drawing-room.

Pipe-smoking is not permitted in any part of the House.

During the meetings of the Club, no smoking is permitted in the rooms in which the meetings are held.

IV.

DOGS.

No dog shall be allowed in the Club House.

V.

GAMES.

No game shall be played in the Club House on Sunday.

VI.

COMPLAINTS.

Complaints of any deficiency in the service of the Club, of over-charges, mischarges, mistakes, or defects, must be made in writing to the House Committee only.

VII.

DINING-ROOM.

No member shall bring into the dining-room between the hours of five and seven P.M. more than one person who has not a card of invitation to the Club.

LIST OF OFFICERS AND MEMBERS.

FORMER PRESIDENTS, TREASURERS AND SECRETARIES.

Presidents.

EDWARD EVERETT	1863–1865
CHARLES G. LORING	1866–1867
RICHARD H. DANA	1868–1870
HENRY LEE	1871
ENOCH R. MUDGE	1872–1874
LEMUEL SHAW	1875–1879
ROBERT W. HOOPER	1880–1881
WILLIAM G. RUSSELL	1882–1884

Treasurers.

SAMUEL G. WARD	1863
FRANCIS E. PARKER	1864
JOHN C. ROPES	1865
THORNTON K. LOTHROP	1866
ARTHUR J. C. SOWDON	1867
GEORGE B. CHASE	1868–1870
JOSIAH F. GUILD	1871–1873
ALFRED B. HILL	1874–1879
WILLIAM P. KUHN	1880–1884

Secretaries.

CHARLES W. STOREY	1863
ROBERT E. APTHORP	1864–1867
LEMUEL SHAW	1868–1869
JAMES C. DAVIS	1870–1874
CHARLES E. STRATTON	1875–1881

OFFICERS FOR 1885.

COMMITTEE ON ELECTIONS.

HENRY LEE, CHAIRMAN

HENRY P. BOWDITCH

GEORGE B. CHASE

CHARLES DEVENS

ALFRED D. FOSTER

CHARLES C. JACKSON

GEORGE P. KING

CALEB WM. LORING

HENRY PARKMAN

EDWARD B. ROBINS

DANIEL SARGENT

S. LOTHROP THORNDIKE

HENRY VAN BRUNT

ROGER WOLCOTT

HENRY W. SWIFT, *Secretary.*

RESIDENT MEMBERS.

Ernestus William Bowditch 1879

Henry Pickering Bowditch 1863

Jonathan Ingersoll Bowditch 1863

George Hillard Bradford 1882

Thomas Gamaliel Bradford 1863

John Frederick Flemmich Brewster 1884

William Brewster 1885

Lincoln Flagg Brigham 1864

Martin Brimmer 1863

Edward Brooks 1881

Francis Brooks 1863

Henry Brooks 1883

Edward Jackson Brown 1874

Francis Perkins Browne 1864

Henry Bryant 1881

John Bryant 1881

Henry Hall Buck 1882

Howard Mendenhall Buck 1884

James McKeller Bugbee 1874

Nathan Willis Bumstead 1865

Robert Manton Burnett 1877

Benjamin Franklin Butler 1863

Arthur Tracy Cabot 1884

Benjamin Shreve Calef 1872

George Hyland Campbell 1875

John Wilson Candler. 1863

William Latham Candler 1865

Edward Montagu Cary 1864

Horace Parker Chandler 1872

Parker Cleaveland Chandler 1876

Peleg Whitman Chandler 1863

Walter Channing 1885

Horace Dwight Chapin 1885

John Henry Chapman 1882

George Bigelow Chase 1863

George Harvey Chickering . . 1865

Charles Francis Choate 1863

George Albert Clark 1866

Alexander Cochrane . . . 1882

Hugh Cochrane 1881

Charles Russell Codman 1863

George Winthrop Coffin 1863

Harrison Gray Otis Colby 1884

Horace Hopkins Coolidge 1863

Joseph Randolph Coolidge 1863

Charles White Copeland 1877

Charles Edward Cotting 1879

Charles Uriah Cotting 1864

George Glover Crocker 1877

Uriel Haskell Crocker 1874

John Cummings 1873

Edward Francis Daland 1865

Charles Henry Dalton 1863

Henry Rogers Dalton 1880

Isaac Warren Danforth 1863

Bancroft Chandler Davis 1885

George Gilbert Davis 1884

James Clarke Davis 1866

Joseph Muenscher Day 1865

Thomas White Deland 1875

Hasket Derby 1864

Charles Devens 1863

Franklin Gordon Dexter 1863

Frederic Dexter 1881

George Dickenson . . 1865

John Calvin Dodge 1863

Ellerton Lodge Dorr 1868

George William Webster Dove 1873

Eben Sumner Draper 1885

George Draper 1865

George Albert Draper 1885

William Franklin Draper 1881

Loren Griswold DuBois . 1882

William Frederic Duff 1877

Thomas Dunnell 1878

Henry Dorr Dupee 1885

William Richardson Dupee 1868

Benjamin Franklin Dwight 1863

Edmund Dwight 1863

Louis Dyer 1882

James Thomas Eldredge 1865

John Wheelock Elliot 1882

William Rogers Ellis 1879

Nathaniel Henry Emmons 1864

George Munroe Endicott . 1879

William Endicott, Jr. 1863

William Ellery Channing Eustis 1882

William Everett 1863

Charles Francis Fairbanks . . . 1875

William Gilson Farlow 1882

Charles Frederick Farrington 1867

Clement Kelsey Fay 1884

Benjamin Faxon Field	1865
Benjamin Faxon Field, Jr.	1878
Walbridge Abner Field	1864
Eustace Carey Fitz	1875
Desmond FitzGerald	1880
George Luther Foote	1868
John Murray Forbes	1863
William Hathaway Forbes	1863
Edward Jacob Forster	1874
Alfred Dwight Foster	1873
Burnside Foster	1883
Charles Henry Wheelwright Foster	1882
Charles Orin Foster	1865
Nathaniel Foster, Jr.	1863
Charles Francis	1864
Horace Vinton Freeman	1879
James Goldthwait Freeman	1870
Aaron Davis Weld French	1868
John Davis Williams French	1868
Lyman Pruden French	1874
William Abrams French	1879
Henry Walker Frost	1870
Robert Oliver Fuller	1872

William Sewall Gardner 1881

William Gaston 1864

Joseph Mackean Gibbens 1863

Horatio James Gilbert 1867

Frederick Huntington Gillett 1879

Daniel Angell Gleason 1863

John Murray Glidden 1864

George Augustus Goddard . . 1869

William Benjamin Goldsmith . 1882

George Henry Gordon 1866

Richard Hinckley Gorham . . 1881

Horace Gray 1863

William Gray, Jr. 1865

John Orne Green 1869

George William Gregerson 1879

Merriweather Hood Griffith 1871

William Oren Grover 1863

Charles Fox Guild 1874

Frederick Guild, Jr. 1879

George Augustine Haines 1873

George Silsbee Hale 1863

Henry Larned Hallett 1863

Richard Price Hallowell 1863

Asa Gustavus Hapgood   1881

Edgar Harding   1880

Herbert Lee Harding   1881

Alpheus Holmes Hardy   1872

George Ropes Harris   1884

William Tennant Hart   1875

William Cushing Haskins   1875

Franklin Haven, Jr.   1865

Edward Daniel Hayden   1866

Henry Williamson Haynes   1878

Charles Dudley Head   1863

Robert Carter Heaton   1877

Alfred Hemenway   1884

John Augustus Higginson   1863

Waldo Higginson   1863

Clement Hugh Hill   1865

Hamilton Andrews Hill   1865

James Edward Radford Hill   1885

Edwin Augustus Hills   1880

William Hilton   1863

Howard Hinckley   1881

Ebenezer Rockwood Hoar   1863

Samuel Hoar   1878

John Hogg   1874

George Henry Homans 1863

John Homans . . 1882

Edward William Hooper 1864

John Prentiss Hopkinson . 1881

Charles Paine Horton 1867

Henry Stone Hovey . 1866

Elmer Parker Howe . . 1882

James Murray Howe, Jr. . . 1878

James Frothingham Hunnewell . . . 1865

Charles Whiting Huntington . . 1863

Francis William Hurd . 1864

Charles Lewis Hutchins 1880

Constantine Foundoulaki Hutchins . . 1880

Henry Clinton Hutchins . . . 1868

Charles Cabot Jackson . . . 1867

Edward Jackson 1863

Frank Jackson 1881

Arthur Earl Jones . 1881

Walter Ingersoll Jones . . 1878

Charles Archibald Kidder . . 1882

Henry Purkitt Kidder 1863

Nathaniel Thayer Kidder . 1885

George Parsons King 1865
Lincoln Newton Kinnicutt 1885
William Putnam Kuhn . . . 1865

Horatio Appleton Lamb . 1881
William Thomas Lambert 1884
John Lathrop 1867
Daniel Warren Lawrence 1881
Elliot Cabot Lee 1883
Francis Wilson Lee 1879
Henry Lee . . 1863
McPherson LeMoyne 1880
Arthur Lincoln 1877
Solomon Lincoln 1876
Thomas Leonard Livermore . . 1880
Henry Cabot Lodge 1879
Harry Vinton Long 1882
John Davis Long 1877
Caleb William Loring . 1863
William Caleb Loring 1879
Thornton Kirkland Lothrop . . . 1863
John Lowell 1863
John Lowell, Jr. 1882
John Dandridge Henley Luce . . 1879

George Hinckley Lyman 1883

John Pickering Lyman .   .   1879

Henry Lyon 1875

Thomas Mack 1863

Edward Benjamin Maltby . 1882

Austin Agnew Martin . 1881

Henry McLean Martin 1876

Frederick Mason 1873

Mortimer Blake Mason . . 1883

William Frederick Matchett 1870

Frederick Warren Goddard May   . 1863

William Walker McKim . 1881

James Henry McMullan .   . 1869

William Andrew Mehaffey 1881

James Morris Meredith 1882

Charles Merriam 1881

Frank Merriam   1875

Herbert Merriam .   . . 1867

Arthur Mills 1881

Richard Sweet Milton 1866

Thomas Minns 1869

William Minot, Jr. 1876

Henry Lee Morse 1881

Robert McNeil Morse, Jr. 1867

Samuel Torrey Morse 1863

David Nevins 1882

Benjamin White Nichols 1863

Lyman Nichols 1874

George Augustus Nickerson . 1882

Frederick Russell Nourse . . . 1880

Henry Kemble Oliver, Jr. . 1868

Joseph Pearson Oliver . . 1881

Francis Augustus Osborn . . 1865

George Laurie Osgood . . . 1877

James Ripley Osgood . 1866

John Felt Osgood . . 1871

Walter Joseph Otis . 1884

Charles Jackson Paine 1866

Robert Treat Paine . 1863

Ebenezer Francis Parker . . 1865

Edmund Morley Parker . 1883

Francis Edward Parker . . . 1863

William Lincoln Parker . . 1879

John Parkinson 1867

Francis Parkman .	1863
Henry Parkman . .	1879
Gilbert Russell Payson	1863
Samuel Russell Payson . . .	1863
Frank Everett Peabody .	1881
Oliver White Peabody	1865
Charles Callahan Perkins . . .	1869
George Hamilton Perkins . .	1880
George Gorham Peters . . .	1884
Willard Peele Phillips	1863
Henry Lillie Pierce . .	1863
Jacob Willard Pierce . .	1877
Alexander Sylvanus Porter	1868
Edward Ellerton Pratt . . .	1866
John Carroll Pratt .	1863
Thomas Parker Proctor	1876
George Putnam	1863
Edmund Quincy	1867
Henry Parker Quincy	1865
Josiah Quincy . . .	1884
Samuel Miller Quincy	1869
James Russell Reed .	1884

John Reed	1866
Alexander Hamilton Rice . . .	1863
Henry Allen Rice, Jr. .	1878
Francis Cedric Richards . . .	1881
George Henry Richards	1863
William Reuben Richards . .	1885
Thomas Oren Richardson .	1866
William Lambert Richardson .	1875
George Ripley	1875
William Roberts	1873
Edward Blake Robins . . .	1876
Alfred Perkins Rockwell	1870
Henry Munroe Rogers	1874
John Codman Ropes	1864
Matthias Denman Ross .	1863
Waldo Ogden Ross . .	1875
Edward Baldwin Russell .	1874
Le Baron Russell	1863
Thomas Russell	1863
William Goodwin Russell . .	1863
Daniel Waldo Salisbury	1863
William Gurdon Saltonstall	1884
George Partridge Sanger	1863

George Partridge Sanger, Jr. 1882

Daniel Sargent 1867

Horace Binney Sargent, Jr. . 1879

Barthold Schlesinger. . . . 1863

Sebastian Benzon Schlesinger . . 1863

Joshua Montgomery Sears . . . 1879

George Otis Shattuck . . . 1863

Henry Russell Shaw 1883

John Oakes Shaw, Jr. . . . 1880

Robert Gould Shaw . 1882

Samuel Savage Shaw 1866

Harvey Newton Shepard 1880

Edward Sherwin 1881

William Simes 1879

Frank Ernest Simpson . . . 1883

Jacob Henry Sleeper 1868

Edward Melancthon Smith 1870

Francis Hill Smith 1872

Robert Dickson Smith 1871

George Snell 1868

George Henry Snelling 1866

Augustus Lord Soule 1873

Arthur John Clark Sowdon 1864

John Perrin Spaulding 1874

Mahlon Day Spaulding . . .	1882
Edwin Loring Sprague . . .	1879
Henry Harrison Sprague . .	1875
Benjamin Franklin Stevens	1863
Charles Edward Stevens	1873
Charles Storrow . .	1864
Charles Storer Storrow . . .	1863
Charles Edwin Stratton	1869
Solomon Piper Stratton	1877
George Blake Sullivan	1877
Henry Dorr Sullivan .	1882
Richard Sullivan . .	1863
Thomas Russell Sullivan	1875
Eben Sutton	1870
Paul Mitchell Swain	1878
William Willard Swan	1867
Walter Howard Sweet	1878
Frank Eliot Sweetser . . .	1884
Henry Walton Swift	1879
Lewis William Tappan, Jr.	1867
George Grosvenor Tarbell	1882
George Thacher	1884
Eugene Van Rensselaer Thayer . . .	1881

Nathaniel Thayer . . 1881

John Babson Thomas . . 1885

Albert Harris Thompson . . 1875

Francis Thompson 1872

George Washington Thompson . 1881

Robert Means Thompson . . . 1877

Samuel Lothrop Thorndike . 1863

Joseph Gilbert Thorp, Jr. . . . 1885

Charles Linzee Tilden . . 1868

George Horton Tilden . 1872

David Townsend 1868

Edward Britton Townsend . . 1878

Charles Russell Train . 1866

Samuel Putnam Train . . 1877

Ezra Prentiss Treadwell 1884

Nathaniel Dana Turner 1869

William James Underwood 1872

George Bruce Upton . 1863

Theodore Newton Vail . 1882

Henry Van Brunt . . . 1865

Benjamin Vaughan 1879

William Warren Vaughan 1880

Alexander Fairfield Wadsworth 1867

George Gorham Walbach 1885

Henry Pickering Walcott 1880

Nathaniel Wales 1877

Francis Amasa Walker 1882

Henshaw Bates Walley 1864

Isaac Chapman Bates Walley . . . 1880

Samuel Dennis Warren 1863

William Warren 1871

Alexander Calvin Washburn . 1863

Francis Sedgwick Watson . . 1882

Robert Sedgwick Watson 1863

William Edward Welch . . 1880

Benjamin Rodman Weld . 1870

Charles Goddard Weld . . . 1884

Otis Everett Weld 1866

William Fletcher Weld . 1882

Samuel Wells . . 1870

Henry Clay Weston . . . 1881

Alexander Strong Wheeler . . 1877

Henry Wheeler 1885

Edmund March Wheelwright . 1882

George William Wheelwright . 1884

John Tyler Wheelwright 1882

John William Wheelwright . .   1868

Charles Goddard White   1878

Charles Joyce White 1875

Harold Whiting   1885

Henry Whitman .   1870

William Henry Whitmore . .   . 1867

Edward Herbert Whitney .   1865

Henry Austin Whitney .   . 1867

William Fiske Whitney 1878

David Weld Williams   . . . 1882

Jacob Lafayette Williams .   1871

John Davis Williams   1868

Sydney Augustus Williams . .   1876

William Cross Williamson .   . . 1868

Walter Thaxter Winsor 1880

Roger Wolcott 1882

Edward Stickney Wood 1885

William Barry Wood 1870

Alexander Young 1865

Charles Loring Young 1863

James ᵀᵃ len Young 1884

NON-RESIDENT MEMBERS.

George Potter Barrett 1882

Edward Julius Berwind . . . 1881

Henry Lincoln Breed 1872

Frederick Turner Brown . . 1880

John Marshall Brown 1869

Philip Henry Brown 1877

Ira Bursley 1864

John Church 1875

Joseph Horace Clark 1881

Charles Warren Clifford 1874

Walter Clifford 1874

Francis Davis Cobb 1883

John Lewis Cutler 1875

William Everett Cutter . 1883

Edward Augustus Dana 1876

Edward Livingston Davis 1871

William Wanton Dunnell 1880

Samuel Coffin Eastman 1879

Arthur Brewster Emmons 1880

Francis Fessenden 1882

Henry Greene Bronson Fisher 1883

George Augustus Flagg 1874

John Holmes Goodenow 1880

Francis Bunker Greene 1882

John Greenough 1880

Edmund Grinnell 1878

Clemens Herschel 1880

Alfred Bryce Hill 1866

George Frisbie Hoar 1870

Thomas Sterry Hunt 1872

John LaFarge 1879

Francis Lathrop 1883

George Shattuck Morison 1878

Lewis Pierce 1872

Charles Warner Plummer 1882

Charles Sturtevant Randall 1883

William Rotch Robeson, Jr. 1867

Morgan Rotch 1882

Stephen Salisbury 1870

Joseph Sargent, Jr. 1875

John Schouler 1870

Hamilton Barclay Staples 1872

Titus Salter Tredick 1863
Joseph Curtis Tyler, Jr. 1882
William Robert Ware 1865
John Davis Washburn 1875
Charles Storey Wheelwright 1877
William Dana Wheelwright 1881

Resident Members 451
Non-resident Members 48
Total of Resident and Non-resident Members . . 499

ARMY AND NAVY MEMBERS.

William Crozier

Hamilton Perkins

Charles Walker Raymond

John Franksford Tarbell

Gilbert E. Thornton

Fletcher A. Wilson

www.ingramcontent.com/pod-product-compliance
Lightning Source LLC
Chambersburg PA
CBHW031804090426
42739CB00008B/1149